Meals Around the World

Meals in Turkey

by Cari Meister

Bullfrog Books

Ideas for Parents and Teachers

Bullfrog Books let children practice reading informational text at the earliest reading levels. Repetition, familiar words, and photo labels support early readers.

Before Reading

- Discuss the cover photo. What does it tell them?

- Look at the picture glossary together. Read and discuss the words.

Read the Book

- "Walk" through the book and look at the photos. Let the child ask questions. Point out the photo labels.

- Read the book to the child, or have him or her read independently.

After Reading

- Prompt the child to think more. Ask: Have you ever eaten Turkish food? Were the flavors new to you? What did you like best?

Bullfrog Books are published by Jump!
5357 Penn Avenue South
Minneapolis, MN 55419
www.jumplibrary.com

Library of Congress Cataloging-in-Publication Data

Names: Meister, Cari, author.
Title: Meals in Turkey / by Cari Meister.
Description: Minneapolis, MN: Jump!, Inc. [2017]
Series: Meals around the world | Audience: Ages 5–8.
Audience: K to grade 3. | Includes index.
Identifiers: LCCN 2016013594 (print)
LCCN 2016014581 (ebook)
ISBN 9781620313770 (hardcover: alk. paper)
ISBN 9781620314951 (pbk.)
ISBN 9781624964244 (ebook)
Subjects: LCSH: Food—Turkey—Juvenile literature.
Cooking, Turkish—Juvenile literature.
Food habits—Turkey—Juvenile literature.
Classification: LCC TX725.T8 M45 2017 (print)
LCC TX725.T8 (ebook) | DDC 394.1/209561—dc23
LC record available at http://lccn.loc.gov/2016013594

Editor: Jenny Fretland VanVoorst
Series Designer: Ellen Huber
Book Designer: Leah Sanders
Photo Researchers: Kirsten Chang, Leah Sanders

Photo Credits: All photos by Shutterstock except: Alamy, 10, 12–13, 14, 18–19, 23tr; Dreamstime, 4, 16–17; Getty, 5, 8–9.

Printed in the United States of America at Corporate Graphics in North Mankato, Minnesota.

Table of Contents

At the Pazar

Ada gets up.

She has tea.

She has breakfast with her family.

She has a plate of food.

It has olives.

It has cheese.

It has an egg and honey.

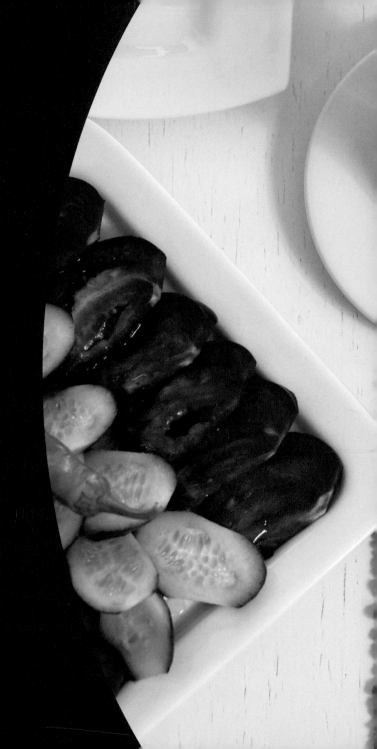

8

Ada and Hud
go to the pazar.

The food is fresh!

They buy black
cabbage.

They buy spices.

Later they will make corba.

Ela is in the city.

It is lunchtime.

The food vendors are busy!

There are many kinds of food.

She sees kumpir.

They are stuffed potatoes.

She sees kofte.

They are meatballs.

She sees kebabs.

kebab

15

Ela sees Berk.

He has a big
hunk of beef.

It is cooking
on a skewer.

"That is what
I want!" she says.

skewer

Berk shaves off
some meat.

He adds tomatoes.

He adds onions.

He puts it in
some bread.

Yum!

Make Kale Corba!

Make this delicious soup from Turkey. Be sure to get an adult to help.

Ingredients:

- 1 bunch kale, washed
- 2 onions, sliced thinly
- 1 cup cooked white navy beans
- ½ cup rice
- 1 tbsp butter
- 1 tbsp olive oil
- 1 tbsp red pepper flakes
- salt and pepper
- 5–6 cups chicken stock

Directions:

❶ Cut kale into thin strips. Discard the white vein in the middle of the leaves.

❷ Put the kale strips in a bowl and salt lightly.

❸ Melt butter and olive oil in saucepan.

❹ Add onion and cook until soft.

❺ Add salted kale to pan and cook until wilted.

❻ Add rice, navy beans, and chicken stock.

❼ Add red pepper flakes, salt, and pepper.

❽ Cook over gentle heat for 30 minutes.

❾ Serve hot.

Picture Glossary

corba
Soup.

kumpir
Baked potatoes stuffed with different fillings.

kebabs
Skewers of meat and vegetables cooked on a grill.

pazar
An open-air marketplace.

kofte
Turkish meatballs.

skewer
A sharp metal rod used for cooking meat over an open flame.

Index

To Learn More

Learning more is as easy as 1, 2, 3.

1) Go to www.factsurfer.com

2) Enter "mealsinTurkey" into the search box.

3) Click the "Surf" button to see a list of websites.

With factsurfer.com, finding more information is just a click away.